THE LITTLE GUIDE TO
BUTTERFLIES

THE LITTLE GUIDE TO
BUTTERFLIES

Illustrations
by Tom Frost

Words by
Alison Davies

quadrille

Introduction

Whether you're new to the world of butterflies or an avid fan, there's no doubt that the mesmerising creatures offered up in these pages will capture your heart. Such a vibrant array of colours, intricate patterns and sheer beauty, portrayed in a collection of prints that encapsulate the essence of each individual butterfly, along with descriptions and interesting facts to bring each image to life. It's no wonder that these insects have fascinated humankind for centuries.

A long-standing symbol of transformation, a butterfly goes through a huge process of change, metamorphosing from egg to larva, then pupa (also called chrysalis) and finally emerging fully formed. It may look delicate but it has the strength to withstand each change and a number of other adaptations that serve it well in its short lifespan. In mythology throughout the world, the butterfly represents the soul and its journey in this life and the next. It appears on Christian tombs and in artwork, and also features in folklore. In ancient Greece the goddess Psyche, whose name translates as 'soul', is often depicted as a butterfly or a beautiful woman with butterfly wings. The Native Americans consider the butterfly a symbol of good fortune, and some tribes believe they bring the blessing of sleep and peaceful dreams. The butterfly is one of nature's wonders, each species with its own unique behaviour patterns.

In this book you will find a treasure trove of information to help you understand these enigmatic creatures, and all the facts you need to explore their world. There's a spotter's guide at the back to help you find and identify all of the butterflies listed and the carefully crafted images give you a sense of the great diversity of the butterfly world.

Welcome to the magical realm of butterflies!

*Just when the caterpillar
thought the world was over,
it became a butterfly.*

ENGLISH PROVERB

European Peacock

Aglais io

WINGSPAN 6.3 to 7.5cm (2½ to 3in)

HABITAT Meadows, fields, gardens and forests

DISTRIBUTION Widespread throughout Europe
and across temperate Asia to Japan

LIFESPAN Up to 11 months (adults hibernate)

MALES AND FEMALES Males and females are similar in
appearance, but the female is slightly larger than the male

This multicoloured gem of a butterfly gets its name
from the stunning eyespots on its wings, which are
thought to scare predators. A fan of many flowering
plants, it can often be found sunning itself on a clump
of dandelions, hemp or wild marjoram. It also feeds
on rotting fruit and tree sap. The male perches high up
to give him the best view of flying females. He'll only
mate with one female at a time, but she is capable of
producing batches of 400 eggs on nettles.

Orange Tip

Anthocharis cardamines

WINGSPAN 4 to 5cm (1⅝ to 2in)
HABITAT Meadows, gardens, riverbanks, hedgerows and woodland glades
DISTRIBUTION Most of Europe
LIFESPAN Around 4 weeks
MALES AND FEMALES Males are white with orange wing tips,
females are also white with dark-grey wing tips

A sign of spring, the Orange Tip emerges in April, indicating that the seasons are finally changing and new growth is afoot. Once called 'the lady of the woods', in Britain, the French and German names *L'Aurore* and *Aurorafalter* also fittingly mean 'rising sun'. The bright orange tips on the male's wings are there to warn off predators, which is just as well as these ethereal creatures contain large amounts of mustard oil from their food plants. This means that although they look fabulous, they taste the opposite.

Purple Emperor

Apatura iris

WINGSPAN 7.5 to 8.5cm (3 to 3⅜in)
HABITAT Dense scrub, woodland areas
DISTRIBUTION Central Europe, parts of Asia, including central and western China
LIFESPAN Up to 3 weeks
MALES AND FEMALES Dark with white-banded wings, males have a purple sheen; females are brown with an orange-ringed eyespot under the forewing

This regal butterfly soars through the treetops and can be hard to spot. At first glance the male looks black and white, but when the sunlight catches his wings a glorious purple-jewelled hue can be seen. This elusive butterfly prefers to perch high up but will come down to earth to feed on the mineral salts in soil, carrion and bird droppings. In folklore around the world butterflies are linked to the human soul and purple butterflies, like the *Apatura iris,* are especially significant. They represent courage, faith and royalty, making the Purple Emperor the perfect name for this creature.

Amazon Beauty

Baeotus aeilus

WINGSPAN 7.5cm (3in)
HABITAT Lowland wet tropical forests
DISTRIBUTION Costa Rica to the Amazon basin
LIFESPAN 14 days
MALES AND FEMALES Males have a band of reflective blue scales
on their upperside, while the females are banded with pale orange

Incredibly rare, these beautiful butterflies like to hang
out on riverbanks or anywhere the soil is wet and rich
in mineral salts. They live on a diet of rotten fruit.
In folklore from this region the butterfly is associated
with both fire and water and it's easy to see how the
ancients could draw this conclusion by looking at the
colours and the habitat of these winged creatures.
With its vivid and distinct blue-black upperside and
speckled black-and-white with orange underside, the
Amazon Beauty lives up to its name.

Bhutan Glory

Bhutanitis lidderdalii

WINGSPAN 8.5 to 11cm (3⅜ to 4⅜in)

HABITAT Treetops, hills and ridges

DISTRIBUTION Bhutan, north-eastern parts of India
and south-eastern parts of Asia

LIFESPAN 14 days

MALES AND FEMALES Males and females
are almost identical in appearance

This mysterious swallowtail butterfly has quite a reputation.
Preferring to fly in foggy, wet conditions, folklore suggests it
makes an appearance once a year after a monsoon. A high
flier, it swoops and coasts sedately above the trees, which
means it's the almost transparent, grey underside that is
mostly seen. This view also gives it a ghost-like appearance
as it blends into the canopy above. During the rainy season
it perches on leaves and uses its front wings like a cloak to
conceal any colouration that might reveal its presence.

Holly Blue

Celastrina argiolus

WINGSPAN 2.6 to 3.4cm (1 to 1⅜in)
HABITAT Gardens, woodlands, hedgerows and parks
DISTRIBUTION Eurasia and North America
LIFESPAN 14 days
MALES AND FEMALES Bright blue wings;
females have black wing edges

This pretty blue butterfly emerges before most
other Blues in spring and can often be found
fluttering around bushes and trees. Food plants
include Holly in spring and Ivy in summer; because
of this it is frequently spotted in churchyards, where
both bushes often grow. Numbers of the Holly Blue
fluctuate from year to year, mainly because of the
parasitic ichneumon wasp (*Listrodomus nycthemerus*)
which injects its eggs into the larvae.

Red Lacewing

Cethosia biblis

WINGSPAN 8 to 9cm (3⅛ to 3½in)

HABITAT Sub-tropical hill forests

DISTRIBUTION Indian subcontinent, South-East Asia, East Asia;
also found on the islands of the Philippines, Sumatra, Borneo, Java,
Sulawesi, Bali, Ambon and Serang

LIFESPAN 8 days

MALES AND FEMALES The male has bright orange to red
upperwings with black and white edges; the female's are greyish-
brown with black spots and white bands and spots on black margins

The Red Lacewing gets its name from the intricate lace-like
patterns on the wings, which help to disguise the butterfly's
shape from predators. It is easy to catch sight of the ornate
patterns as it enjoys basking with its wings wide open in the
sunshine. Particularly active first thing in the morning, this
butterfly feeds on the Passion flower (*Passiflora*), a poisonous
climbing plant. Also poisonous, the Red Lacewing's
distinctive colouring acts as a warning to predators.

Monarch

Danaus plexippus

WINGSPAN 9 to 10cm (3½ to 4in)
HABITAT Open fields and meadows
DISTRIBUTION Mexico, North America, and Canada
(a rare migrant to the British Isles)
LIFESPAN Usually up to 5 weeks, but Monarchs born at the end of summer migrate
to Mexico where they remain until spring, living for approximately 8 months
MALES AND FEMALES Males have a black spot at the centre of each hindwing
that is not present in females

Adventurers with wings, some Monarchs migrate thousands of miles each year from Canada to the South of Mexico. They know the direction even though they've never made the journey before, as they have an inner compass that leads the way. One old wives' tale suggests that if you see a swarm of Monarchs, you'll be blessed with sunshine; this is most likely because of the bright orange hue of their wings. Monarchs are poisonous, as the caterpillars feed on Milkweed which builds up toxins in their system that remain into adulthood.

Banded Orange Tiger

Dryadula phaetusa

WINGSPAN 8.6 to 8.9cm (3⅜ to 3½in)

HABITAT Lowland tropical fields and valleys

DISTRIBUTION Brazil, Central America to Central Mexico

LIFESPAN 2 to 3 weeks

MALES AND FEMALES Males, upperside is orange with black stripes; females are duller and the stripes are less defined

Also known as the Banded Orange Heliconian, this bright orange butterfly can occasionally fly as far as Florida in the summer months. Gathering in large groups before the mating season, the males typically feed on mineral salts found in moist soil and mud. Bird droppings are also part of their diet and, if needs be, they will also take the salty secretions from the skin and nasal passages of certain animals.

Tailed Green Jay

Graphium agamemnon

WINGSPAN 8 to 10cm (3⅛ to 4in)

HABITAT Woodland, rainforests, gardens and urban areas

DISTRIBUTION Native to India, Sri Lanka,
through South-East Asia and Australia

LIFESPAN 8 days

MALES AND FEMALES Both species similar but the female has a greenish-white streak which runs along the dorsal margin on both upper and undersides

Often called the Tailed Jay or the Green-Spotted Triangle, this active butterfly continues to flutter its wings whilst feeding on nectar. A strong and agile flier, the spotted apple-green colouring makes it virtually invisible in the rainforest thanks to the way the sunlight filters through the leafy canopy. Although they favour the treetops, adult butterflies can be seen whilst feeding on nectar from flowers such as Poinsettia, Lantana and Mussaenda.

Glasswinged Butterfly

Greta oto

WINGSPAN 5.5 to 6cm (2⅛ to 2⅜in)
HABITAT Rainforest
DISTRIBUTION Central to South America
LIFESPAN 6 to 12 weeks
MALES AND FEMALES Males and females are almost identical

One of nature's miracles, the glasswing, as the name hints, has translucent wings that allow it virtually to disappear into its native rainforest. The only clue that this creature is there is in the dark, often orange, hue that frames its wings beautifully. In Spanish its name is *espejitos* which means 'little mirrors'. The membranes of each wing refract light, distributing an array of colour if caught at the right angle, but when the butterfly is in flight it appears to vanish, making it almost impossible for predators to spot. Despite its delicate appearance, this butterfly's wings are as strong and durable as those of any other species. It flies long distances, sometimes 20 kilometres (12 miles) in a day.

Zebra Longwing

Heliconius charithonia

WINGSPAN 7 to 10cm (2¾ to 4in)

HABITAT Forest settings, subtropical areas, thickets, gardens

DISTRIBUTION Southern portions of the United States southward through Mexico, Central America and the West Indies to South America

LIFESPAN Several months

MALES AND FEMALES Similar in colour and markings

The state butterfly of Florida since 1996, the Zebra Longwing is a striking creature. Medium-sized, it has elongated wings and a vivid striped pattern. It tends to roost in groups of around 50 adults and has developed a pecking order with the oldest getting the best roosting spots. Although not easily startled, it does make an eerie creaking sound if disturbed, by wriggling its entire body. The Zebra Longwing follows a set foraging route to its favourite food plants – Shepherd's Needle and Lantana – and it eats pollen as well as nectar.

Sapho Longwing

Heliconius sapho

WINGSPAN 7.5 to 8.8cm (3 to 3½in)

HABITAT The canopy of tropical rainforests

DISTRIBUTION Native to Central America through to north-western South America

LIFESPAN Up to 7 or 8 weeks

MALES AND FEMALES Male and females are similar in appearance

The name 'Sapho' is thought to derive from the mythological Queen Sapho, rather than the more famous poet Sappho. With their dazzling petrol-blue wings, these butterflies feed on pollen as well as nectar, which lengthens their lifespan from days to weeks. The adults roost in large groups on branches over water and are usually spotted in dense canopy. The Sapho Longwing emanates a sweet scent; this seemingly magical ability is thanks to a special gland in its abdomen.

Gladiator Butterfly

Hypolimnas dexithea

WINGSPAN Around 10cm (4in)
HABITAT Rainforest
DISTRIBUTION A native of Madagascar
LIFESPAN 14 days
MALES AND FEMALES Males and females
are almost identical in appearance

This striking butterfly with its vivid colouration was targeted by collectors shortly after it was discovered. It is now rare and usually only found in Madagascar or in private art collections. The wings have tiny spikes along the edge, something which is unique to the species, and fine scales on the wings create its distinctive ultraviolet patterns. These are used to attract a mate.

Common Buckeye

Junonia coenia

WINGSPAN 4 to 7.5cm (1⅝ to 3in)

HABITAT Open landscapes, fields, roadsides, gardens, parks

DISTRIBUTION Southern United States and Mexico

LIFESPAN Up to 10 days

MALES AND FEMALES Both sexes are similar
but the female is usually larger than the male

This eye-catching American butterfly is easily recognisable
for its distinctive target spots which look like eyes. It cleverly
blends in with its environment depending on the time of year.
In the spring and summer, when plants are new and brighter
in colour, the underside of the wings is lighter and acts as
camouflage. In autumn and winter, the underside turns much
darker to match the landscape. Males tend to form patrols
when looking for a mate, but if a female buckeye decides she's
not interested she'll lift her abdomen into the air. To onlookers
this appears as though she's actively seeking attention, but in
this position it's impossible for him to mate with her.

Blue Pansy

Junonia orithya

WINGSPAN 4 to 5.5cm (1⅜ to 2⅛in)
HABITAT Open grassy wasteland, parks and fields
DISTRIBUTION Native to Africa and found
in Southern parts of Asia and Australia
LIFESPAN 14 days
MALES AND FEMALES The males have bright blue
hindwings and the females have a brown upperside

This sun-loving butterfly can be seen visiting tiny flowers and gliding through the air at speeds of around 12 miles per hour. All butterflies are cold-blooded, which means they cannot regulate their body temperature, so you'll often find them basking in the sun with wide-open wings. Although it might look as though they're sunbathing for pleasure, this practice is essential as the veins in the wings absorb heat and carry it to the rest of the body.

Red-Spotted Purple

Limenitis arthemis astyanax

WINGSPAN 7.5 to 8.5cm (3 to 3⅜in)
HABITAT Forests and woodlands
DISTRIBUTION Native to North America
LIFESPAN 14 days
MALES AND FEMALES Both sexes are identical in
colouration, but the female is slightly larger than the male

This brush-footed butterfly mimics another species, the
Pipevine Swallowtail (*Battus philenor*), a practice that
has evolved so that the Red-Spotted Purple can deflect
predators. Related to the White Admiral butterfly (*Limenitis
camilla*), its bright colours act as further protection from
predators. This butterfly can often be seen on the edges of
woodland or in nearby parks. It rests on shrubs and trees,
gently opening and closing its wings to give those lucky
enough the chance to see its glorious hues.

Marbled White

Melanargia galathea

WINGSPAN 5.3 to 5.8cm (2⅛ to 2¼in)
HABITAT Grasslands, woodland clearings, roadside verges
DISTRIBUTION Most of Europe, South Russia, Asia Minor and Iran
LIFESPAN 2 to 3 months
MALES AND FEMALES Similar colouring but males are purer white
and their underside is grey; females' underside is greyish brown

With its slow, distinctive flight and beautiful black-and-white pattern, it's hard to mistake a Marbled White. Interestingly, despite its name, it belongs to a family of 'Browns' known as *Satyrinae*. Most often seen fluttering above tall grasses or feeding on purple flowers, this striking butterfly's favourite nectar plants are wild marjoram, knapweeds, thistles and brambles. Although grassland is its habitat of choice, it can occasionally be spotted in gardens.

Emperor

Morpho peleides

WINGSPAN 12 to 16cm (4¾ to 6¼in)

HABITAT Rainforests

DISTRIBUTION Mexico, Central America, northern South America, Paraguay and Trinidad

LIFESPAN Around 3 months

MALES AND FEMALES The males' wings are broader and brighter in colour than the females'

Also known as the Blue Morpho Butterfly, the Emperor knows exactly how to make its predators quiver. Gathering in large mobs, it rapidly flashes its startling, iridescent blue wings to scare them away. Unlike other butterflies, the Emperor doesn't feed on nectar from flowers – it prefers tree sap. It has also been known to drink the juice of rotting mangoes, kiwis and lychees. This majestic butterfly prefers to fly in open spaces and can be seen at forest edges, by rivers or on trail paths.

Chimaera Birdwing

Ornithoptera chimaera

WINGSPAN 8 to 18cm (3⅛ to 7in) in females,
7 to 15cm (2¾ to 6in) in males
HABITAT Rainforests and damp gorges
DISTRIBUTION Papua New Guinea, Irian Jaya, Indonesia
LIFESPAN Up to 12 months
MALES AND FEMALES Males are black, green and gold;
females are larger, mostly dark brown, with white and black spots

It's difficult to catch sight of these rare and beautiful butterflies because they tend to fly high in the rainforest canopy. An endangered species because of habitat destruction, Chimaera Birdwings are Swallowtails without the usual tail-like extensions to their hind wings. In Greek mythology, the Chimaera is a fire-breathing she-monster with a lion's head, goat's body and serpent's tail. This creation brought chaos, fire and destruction to the land, quite the opposite to this butterfly seriously threatened by the decline of its environment.

Cairns Birdwing

Ornithoptera euphorion

WINGSPAN 12 to 18cm (4¾ to 7in)
HABITAT Rainforest
DISTRIBUTION North-eastern Australia from Mackay to Cooktown
LIFESPAN 4 to 5 weeks
MALES AND FEMALES The males are green, gold and black;
females are larger and black and white with some yellow markings

This giant of the rainforest is the largest native butterfly in Australia. The females are larger than the males, with some reaching a massive 18cm (7in) wingspan. These ingenious butterflies lay their eggs on vines in the rainforest by using receptors in their legs and abdomen to sense the best and most nutritious leaves. Adults mate quickly, with males taking a military-style approach to hunt for females. The mating process can be vigorous, but the females cleverly release a sedative to calm the male's ardour!

Richmond Birdwing

Ornithoptera richmondia

WINGSPAN Up to 13cm (5in) in males and 16cm (6in) in females
HABITAT Sub-tropical rainforest and gardens
DISTRIBUTION Australia
LIFESPAN 4 to 6 weeks
MALES AND FEMALES Males are striking black and green with a
bright-red splash on the thorax; females are dark brownish with white,
cream or yellowish markings in the hindwing

This beautiful birdwing is one of Australia's largest
butterflies. Although active throughout the day, they're
usually spotted early in the morning or late in the afternoon,
gliding through forests or in gardens. They're attracted to
vibrant blooms and will feed on flowers like *Buddleia*, *Pentas*,
Bauhinia, Honeysuckle and *Impatiens*. Threats to this butterfly's
survival include loss of habitat and the introduction of a
non-native vine, Dutchman's pipe (*Aristolochia elegans*). Any
Richmond Birdwing eggs laid on this vine are doomed as the
plant is highly toxic and kills all the caterpillars.

Crimson Rose

Pachliopta hector

WINGSPAN 9 to 11cm (3½ to 4⅜in)

HABITAT Lowland rainforests, woodlands,
farmland, city parks and gardens

DISTRIBUTION India and Sri Lanka

LIFESPAN From a few weeks to a year

MALES AND FEMALES Males and females are almost identical

With its striking red body and head, it's easy to see
why this swallowtail was named the Crimson Rose. An
adaptable butterfly, the Rose wanders far and wide
and feeds on the nectar of a range of wild flowers. At
the height of migration it is common to see several
thousand gathered together before they embark on their
journey. The second part of the Latin name, '*hector*', is
a nod to the Greek hero and Trojan prince Hector. He
was known as the greatest warrior of Troy, a character
not unlike this butterfly, who thrived in his environment.

Common Lime Butterfly

Papilio demoleus

WINGSPAN 8 to 10cm (3 to 4in)

HABITAT Gardens, parks, semi evergreen and evergreen forests, riverbeds

DISTRIBUTION Widespread throughout the Middle East, Asia, Australia, Caribbean, Central America

LIFESPAN 6 days

MALES AND FEMALES Similar colouration and patterns but the female is usually larger with a greyish-brown underside; male underside is grey

This may be a swallowtail butterfly but unlike the others, it lacks a prominent tail. Sometimes also called the Lemon Butterfly or Small Citrus Butterfly, the names hint at its favourite food source – citrus fruit, in particular the Key Lime plant (*Citrus × aurantiifolia*). Considered a pest, this aggressive butterfly has several modes of flight depending on the time of day. In the morning, flight is slow and laboured; as the day continues it picks up speed and flies low to the ground. At the hottest time of the day it's usually found resting on wet patches on the ground. A common visitor to gardens, it enjoys basking on aromatic herbs and flowers.

Eastern Tiger Swallowtail

Papilio glaucus

WINGSPAN 8 to 14cm (3 to 5½in)

HABITAT Woodlands, fields, creeks, gardens, roadsides

DISTRIBUTION North America

LIFESPAN Around 2 weeks

MALES AND FEMALES The male is yellow with four black tiger stripes on each forewing; females are dimorphic and can be yellow with a band of blue spots or almost completely black

The Eastern Tiger Swallowtail, aptly named for its colour and tiger-like stripes, has adapted well to almost any terrain and has been known to stray into urban areas. A super-strong flier, this butterfly produces two or three broods a year. The males are often seen in large groups mud-puddling, where they gather in muddy puddles to collect nutrients. This swallowtail's favourite nectar plants include Honeysuckle, Azaleas, Milkweed and Thistles, although it will feed on many other species including Magnolias and Cottonwoods.

Jamaican Giant Swallowtail

Papilio homerus

WINGSPAN Average of 15cm (6in)
HABITAT Remote areas with difficult terrain, wet limestone forests
DISTRIBUTION Jamaica
LIFESPAN 5 to 6 months
MALES AND FEMALES The females are larger
and have more yellow on their wing patterns than the males

The largest swallowtail butterfly in the Western Hemisphere, this beauty is under threat from habitat loss and collecting. It inhabits isolated areas, mainly in the mountains of Eastern Jamaica where the male butterflies can grow up to 75mm (3in). A gentle giant, this peaceful creature feeds on the leaves of trees and flowers. Scientists are working out how best to conserve this flagship species in the wild.

Alpine Black Swallowtail

Papilio maackii

WINGSPAN 12 to 14cm (4¾ to 5½in)
HABITAT Forest borders, grasslands and by the coast
DISTRIBUTION Japan, Asia, South Korea, China
LIFESPAN 21 days
MALES AND FEMALES Both sexes have iridescent wings;
the female colouring is more intense

The Alpine Black Swallowtail is known for its gorgeous shimmering wings. The first part of its Japanese name, *Miyama*, means 'mountain beauty', but it's usually spotted at the edge of thick vegetation, hovering near Azalea bushes. Its food of choice is the nectar of the Mikan tree, but it also feeds from other fruit trees such as the Mandarin. In Japanese folklore, the butterfly is associated with good luck in love and is thought to represent a happy marriage between soulmates. Alpine Blacks reinforce this idea by performing an elaborate courtship dance to secure a mate and can often be seen flying in tandem through the sky.

Spicebush Swallowtail

Papilio troilus

WINGSPAN 9 to 12.5cm (3½ to 5in)
HABITAT Woodland, parks, fields, gardens and verges
DISTRIBUTION North America
LIFESPAN 2 days to 2 weeks
MALES AND FEMALES The median areas of the hind wings are dusted with blue in females and blue-green to green in males

Unlike other swallowtail butterflies, the Spicebush prefers to fly low to the ground rather than gliding high up. It takes its name from its caterpillar's favourite host plant, the Spicebush (*Lindera benzoin*). These butterflies take nectar from a range of plants including Honeysuckle, Jewelweed, Thistles and Lantana. In a bid to win their ideal mate, males will perform an elaborate courtship dance. The males also emit powerful pheromones during this intricate display which helps them win suitable partners.

Apollo

Parnassius apollo

WINGSPAN 7 to 8.5cm (2¾ to 3¼in)

HABITAT Hills, alpine meadows, mountainous regions

DISTRIBUTION Spain, France, Italy, Alps, Carpathians, southern Germany, the Balkans, southern Scandinavia (except Denmark), southern Poland and Slovakia

LIFESPAN 2 to 3 weeks

MALES AND FEMALES Male has a yellow-orange line of markings on the upperwing; female has patches of orange

A voracious feeder, this butterfly can often be approached when it's feasting on nectar. Rather than land gracefully, it often crashes into flower heads in its eagerness for nourishment. With stunning colouration and glossy wings, the reddish spots in adults tend to fade in the sun, turning a burnt-orange shade, which makes it easy to distinguish older butterflies. Males are often more active, traversing the slopes while females conserve energy and prefer to settle on the ground, on thistles or stones.

Clipper

Parthenos sylvia

WINGSPAN 10 to 12.5cm (4 to 5in)
HABITAT Evergreen forests
DISTRIBUTION South and South-East Asia
LIFESPAN 2 to 3 weeks
MALES AND FEMALES Identical in colouration

A powerful and fast-flying butterfly, the clipper tends to flap its wings rapidly in a flickering movement, giving it a staccato appearance that stands out from the crowd. Preferring to glide for short periods over treetops near water, it can often be seen flying in large groups. This gorgeous patterned butterfly is pale blue if it comes from Malaysia, or a brownish-yellow shade in other parts of Asia. Its food of choice is the nectar from flowers of the *Adenia* plant, which belongs to the Passion flower family (*Passifloraceae*).

Eastern Comma

Polygonia comma

WINGSPAN 4.5 to 6.5cm (1¾ to 2½in)

HABITAT Woodland, marshes, swamps and near rivers

DISTRIBUTION Eastern North America

LIFESPAN 14 days

MALES AND FEMALES Underside of male is mottled; the underside of the female is an even yellow–brown–grey in shade

This small North American butterfly has two forms: in the summer its hindwing is mostly black, in the winter it's orange with black spots. Both forms have a silvery spot in the centre of the hindwing that resembles a comma. The males can be aggressive, particularly in the hunt for a mate, and have been known to chase other insects and birds. This butterfly has a varied diet, feeding on flowers, rotting fruit, sap, and mineral deposits in the soil and in manure.

Zebra Swallowtail

Protographium marcellus

WINGSPAN 6.5 to 10cm (2½ to 4in)
HABITAT Woodlands near swamps and rivers, savannas and prairies
DISTRIBUTION Native to Eastern United States and Canada
LIFESPAN Up to 6 months
MALES AND FEMALES Similar in colour and markings

The Zebra Swallowtail is easy to distinguish with its triangular-shaped wings and sharp, sword-like tail wings, which extend outwards like two spears. Its name comes from the distinctive black-and-white stripes, but it also has a red stripe running along the ventral hindwing. This butterfly feeds on nectar from flowers including Verbena, Blueberry, Lilac and Common Milkweed, and lays its eggs on shrubs in the Paw Paw (*Asimina*) genus. The females take a slow and steady approach when it comes to flying and sourcing foods, while the males are more direct, flying swiftly to alight on plants and flowerheads.

Rusty-Tipped Page

Siproeta epaphus

WINGSPAN 7 to 7.5cm (2¾ to 3in)

HABITAT Tropical rainforests at high altitude

DISTRIBUTION Central and South America
(Mexico to Peru)

LIFESPAN 21 days

MALES AND FEMALES The males and
females are identical in colouring

Also known as the Brown Siproeta, the Rusty-Tipped
Page gets its name from the burnt-amber wingtips
which are thought to keep predators at bay. These
colourful sun-lovers are usually spotted in small
groups, flying steadily over riverbanks and forest
clearings. Males can be seen on damp roads and
rock faces, flitting from spot to spot in search of
moisture. They feed on the nectar of flowers such as
Impatiens and Lantana, and rotting fruit and carrion.

Malachite

Siproeta stelenes

WINGSPAN 8 to 10cm (3⅛ to 4in)
HABITAT Rainforests, deciduous forests, riverbanks, orchards and gardens
DISTRIBUTION Central to northern South America, Cuba, Brazil
LIFESPAN 30 days
MALES AND FEMALES Males have bright green wings with black stripes, ovals and rectangles; females have similar patterns but are a lighter shade

A truly beautiful butterfly, the Malachite gets its name from the stunning green mineral malachite that also catches the light because it contains copper compounds. Sometimes called the Pearly Malachite, the adult males are often seen in groups roosting on the lower leaves of plants and shrubs. They patrol the air for mates and feast on rotting fruit, flower nectar and bat dung. In the Middle Ages, people believed that wearing or carrying a piece of malachite would protect them from the 'evil eye'. Even today, some believe that this stone can alleviate the fear of flying. This magnificent butterfly of the same name would most likely agree!

Red Pierrot

Talicada nyseus

WINGSPAN 3 to 3.5cm (1⅛ to 1⅜in)
HABITAT Semi-evergreen forests or patches of land, gardens
DISTRIBUTION Indian sub-continent and South-East Asia
LIFESPAN 14 days
MALES AND FEMALES Both sexes are similar in colouration; the females are slightly paler

This striking butterfly is mostly black with white spots at the margins and a bright orange to red band on the lower portion of its hindwings. The underwings are striking white with black markings and an orange band. Small in size, it's noted for its weak flight. It tends to fly in short bursts, basking with half-open wings in shady spots where there is plenty of undergrowth. Its food of choice is Kalanchoe, a tropical flowering plant, but it also likes herbs and other flowers.

Kaiser-i-Hind Swallowtail

Teinopalpus imperialis

WINGSPAN 9 to 12cm (3½ to 4¾in)

HABITAT High-altitude forests, mountainous woodland

DISTRIBUTION Nepal, North India and
east to northern parts of Vietnam

LIFESPAN A week to a year

MALES AND FEMALES The females are larger and
their markings and colouration differ from the males

One of the rarest and most elusive swallowtail butterflies, the Kaiser-i-Hind name means 'Emperor of India'. With a strong, rapid flight and a tendency to seek the solace of the highest treetops, it can be difficult to spot. The males, which can be violently territorial, sometimes alight and settle on plants and stones, but it's rare to catch sight of a female. Males will suck moisture from any wet patches they find on the land and from leaves. Although it is protected by law in India and Nepal, the future of this butterfly is threatened by collectors.

Rajah Brooke's Birdwing

Trogonoptera brookiana

WINGSPAN 15 to 17cm (6 to 6¾in)

HABITAT Tropical rainforests

DISTRIBUTION Malaysia, Borneo and Sumatra,
including some offshore islands

LIFESPAN 14 days

MALES AND FEMALES The males are mainly black with
a chain of vivid green triangular spots on the forewings;
females are mostly brown, with some white and green

It's no surprise that this dazzling butterfly was named after the
White Rajah of Sarawak, Captain Brooke, who ruled an English
Province in northern Borneo in the middle of the 19th century.
The males command respect: gathering in groups of 70 or
more, they provide a blaze of colour as they drink from puddles
of water. They're also often spotted at riverbanks within the
rainforests. Females are elusive, which means the males have to
make an effort to mate with them, often chasing them in mid-
air or ambushing them at an opportune moment.

Golden Birdwing

Troides aeacus

WINGSPAN 15 to 16cm (6 to 6¼in)

HABITAT Rainforest

DISTRIBUTION Northern India, Nepal, Burma, China, Thailand, Laos, Vietnam, Taiwan, Cambodia, peninsular Malaysia and Indonesia

LIFESPAN 4 to 6 weeks

MALES AND FEMALES The male Birdwing is black with golden hindwings; the females are dark brown and larger than the male

The Golden Birdwing is a large butterfly that belongs to the swallowtail family. It's known for its bright yellow hindwings, which catch the eye in flight. Although it's classed as vulnerable, this Birdwing is fairly common and not generally under threat. It feeds on a number of flowering plants in the Pipevine family (*Aristolochiaceae*).

Australian Painted Lady

Vanessa kershawi

WINGSPAN 5.5cm (2⅛in)
HABITAT Plains, hilltops, almost anywhere
DISTRIBUTION Australia
LIFESPAN Approximately 53 days during summer
MALES AND FEMALES The males and females are almost identical in
colouring, with wings a bright orange and brown colour with white patterns

With gorgeous splashes of colour that look as though they've come
straight from the paint pot, there's more to this vibrant butterfly
than meets the eye. The Australian Painted Lady has a blue tint to
the eyespots on its hindwings. It flies low to the ground, between
1 and 2 metres (3 to 6½ feet) and is strongly migratory, flying
in large numbers from north to south Australia in spring. An
Australian aboriginal tale speaks of a boy who abducts a girl and
keeps her in a cave. To escape, she turns into a colourful butterfly,
not unlike the Painted Lady. This narrative reminds us to appreciate
the beauty of this butterfly before she flies away.

Southern Festoon

Zerynthia polyxena

WINGSPAN 6 to 8cm (2⅜ to 3⅛in)

HABITAT Riverbanks, wetlands, vineyards,
cultivated areas, open spaces, rocky cliffs

DISTRIBUTION Europe (SE France, Italy, eastwards to the Balkans)

LIFESPAN 4 to 5 days

MALES AND FEMALES Females are paler
and have slightly larger wings

A butterfly of early spring, usually spotted in April and May, the Southern Festoon prefers the allure of lush green meadows and open spaces. It can be seen in a wide range of habitats, because it favours a variety of foods which grow in different areas. Its wings boast complex markings, making it stand out from the crowd. In particular, the red spots on its hindwings act as a warning to predators.

Spotter's Guide

This butterfly checklist will help you to identify the 40 butterflies in this book. As you spot each butterfly, check them off to keep a record. Though butterflies can be enjoyed without any special equipment, a pair of binoculars can help you to see their impressive detail. Try to avoid any jerky movements or casting a shadow over settled butterflies as this will startle them.

☐ **European Peacock**

Aglais io (p8)

☐ **Bhutan Glory**

Bhutanitis lidderdalii (p16)

☐ **Holly Blue**

Celastrina argiolus (p18)

☐ **Red Lacewing**

Cethosia biblis (p20)

☐ **Orange Tip**

Anthocharis cardamines (p10)

☐ **Purple Emperor**

Apatura iris (p12)

☐ **Amazon Beauty**

Baeotus aeilus (p14)

☐ **Monarch**

Danaus plexippus (p22)

☐ **Banded Orange Tiger**

Dryadula phaetusa (p24)

☐ **Tailed Green Jay**

Graphium agamemnon (p26)

☐ **Glasswinged Butterfly**

Greta oto (p28)

☐ **Zebra Longwing**

Heliconius charithonia (p30)

☐ **Sapho Longwing**

Heliconius sapho (p32)

☐ **Red-Spotted Purple**

Limenitis arthemis astyanax (p40)

☐ **Marbled White**

Melanargia galathea (p42)

☐ **Emperor**

Morpho peleides (p44)

☐ **Gladiator Butterfly**

Hypolimnas dexithea (p34)

☐ **Common Buckeye**

Junonia coenia (p36)

☐ **Blue Pansy**

Junonia orithya (p38)

☐ **Chimaera Birdwing**

Ornithoptera chimaera (p46)

☐ **Cairns Birdwing**

Ornithoptera euphorion (p48)

☐ **Richmond Birdwing**

Ornithoptera richmondia (p50)

□ **Crimson Rose**

Pachliopta hector (p52)

□ **Common Lime Butterfly**

Papilio demoleus (p54)

□ **Eastern Tiger Swallowtail**

Papilio glaucus (p56)

□ **Apollo**

Parnassius apollo (p64)

□ **Clipper**

Parthenos sylvia (p66)

□ **Eastern Comma**

Polygonia comma (p68)

☐ **Jamaican Giant Swallowtail**

Papilio homerus (p58)

☐ **Alpine Black Swallowtail**

Papilio maackii (p60)

☐ **Spicebush Swallowtail**

Papilio troilus (p62)

☐ **Zebra Swallowtail**

Protographium marcellus (p70)

☐ **Rusty-Tipped Page**

Siproeta epaphus (p72)

☐ **Malachite**

Siproeta stelenes (p74)

☐ **Red Pierrot**
Talicada nyseus (p76)

☐ **Kaiser-i-Hind Swallowtail**
Teinopalpus imperialis (p78)

☐ **Rajah Brooke's Birdwing**
Trogonoptera brookiana (p80)

☐ **Golden Birdwing**
Troides aeacus (p82)

☐ **Australian Painted Lady**
Vanessa kershawi (p84)

☐ **Southern Festoon**
Zerynthia polyxena (p86)

94

TOM FROST
Print Maker

Print maker and illustrator Tom Frost graduated from
Falmouth College of Arts in 2001, returning to his home
town of Bristol to work as an illustrator for a number
of years. He now divides his time between printmaking,
restoring his crumbling Georgian house in rural Wales
and raising a young family. In recent years he has worked
with clients including the V&A, Perry's Cider, Art Angels,
Freight Household Goods, *Selvedge* magazine, Betty &
Dupree, The Archivist and Yorkshire Sculpture Park. His
work highlights a fascination for old matchboxes, stamps,
folk art, tin toys, children's books and the natural world.

PUBLISHING DIRECTOR Sarah Lavelle
CREATIVE DIRECTOR Helen Lewis
EDITOR Harriet Butt
DESIGNER Emily Lapworth
ILLUSTRATOR Tom Frost
WORDS Alison Davies
PRODUCTION Vincent Smith,
Nikolaus Ginelli

First published in 2017 by Quadrille,
an imprint of Hardie Grant Publishing

Quadrille
52–54 Southwark Street
London SE1 1UN
quadrille.com

Reprinted in 2017
10 9 8 7 6 5 4 3 2

Cataloguing in Publication Data: A
catalogue record for this book is available
from the British Library.

ISBN 978 1 78713 034 0
Printed in China